Published by Live Love Learn Books Publishing

www.LiveLoveLearnBooks.com

Why Can't I Go? Copyright © 2016 Kathy Carniero

All rights reserved.

Cover art and illustrations designed by Christine "Tiny" Irizarry.

Printed in the United States of America

ISBN-10:0-9903044-8-5

ISBN- 13:978-0-9903044-8-7

Library of Congress Control Number: 2016903160

All rights reserved, no part of this publication may be reproduced, stored in a retrieval system, or transmitted, in any form or by any means, electronic, mechanical, photocopying, recording, or otherwise without written permission of the author. The scanning, and uploading, and distribution of this book via the Internet or via any other means without permission is illegal and punishable by law. Your support of the author's rights is appreciated.

Autism is a mental condition, present from early childhood. It is characterized by showing difficulty in communicating and forming relationships with other people.

This book will be used to share Dafney's story and to help clear the stigma circling around kids with autism.

I love you so much Dafney. You are the sun to my moon and your beautiful smile brightens my day. Never change.
Your sister,
Dorothy

Thank you Dafney for providing inspiration throughout the years I have known you. You truly are an amazing person. I love you Dafney, keep being you.
Your friend,
Lucy

Hi, my name is Dafney, but my Dad calls me Boo-Boo. I am 11 years old

When I was young, a very nice nurse told me I had Autism.

Even though I still felt like everyone else, some people started to act like there was something wrong with me.

This made me sad...

My sister is a little bit older than me and gets to have a lot of fun. When she gets invited to spend the night at a friend's house, I sometimes wonder, why can't I go?

I like to have fun and laugh just like them. I have manners and know how to obey the rules. I enjoy playing games, eating pizza and watching movies too, just like them!

Do they think my Autism is contagious??

I promise they can't
"catch it."
I promise it won't "rub off"
on them.

Sometimes when I get really excited or scared, I have to be reminded how to control my emotions, but doesn't every kid?

When I have something really important I want to say, I may have trouble getting my words to come out right. This can make me get a little upset. If you give me a minute to gather my thoughts, I promise you won't be disappointed.

My heart is filled with so much love that I want to share it with everyone.

When people find out I have Autism they think I do things wrong, but really, I just do things a little bit different.

Dear readers,

I am Dafney Douglas. I'm 11 years old. Next year I'm going to be in middle school with many of my friends. I love to sing, dance, eat chicken and pizza; but I love my Dad to cook me hamburgers that his Dad taught him to make. I love watching my Dad as he listens to jazz music and watches old time movies.

My sister, Dorothy, has many friends who come and visit her, call her on her phone, or just hang out. She is going to high school next year. My Dad doesn't want me to get older, but I keep telling him I'm not a little kid anymore. He tells me about my grandparents who are in heaven; how they watch over me every day. I tell him that I can't see them but he tells me they can see me.

My Dad told me of a gift that God had blessed me with! That some people do understand why it takes me a little longer to do some things. But I can beat my Dad on the Wii, Play Station, etc... Sometimes I help him with his phone or the computer.

He tells me he is better at using a dictionary than me! I ask him why I need a dictionary if I can spell the word. That's why we have spell check! Then he tells me he is older than the internet. That he's a veteran. That veterans are old soldiers. I ask him what war he fought in, Texas? He just laughs! Me and my Dad have fun every day!

He tells me that God has blessed me with Autism, and that I have a lot of love to share with people who want to be my friends. Well, that's just a little about me. I hope you get a better understanding of children with special needs.

Dafney

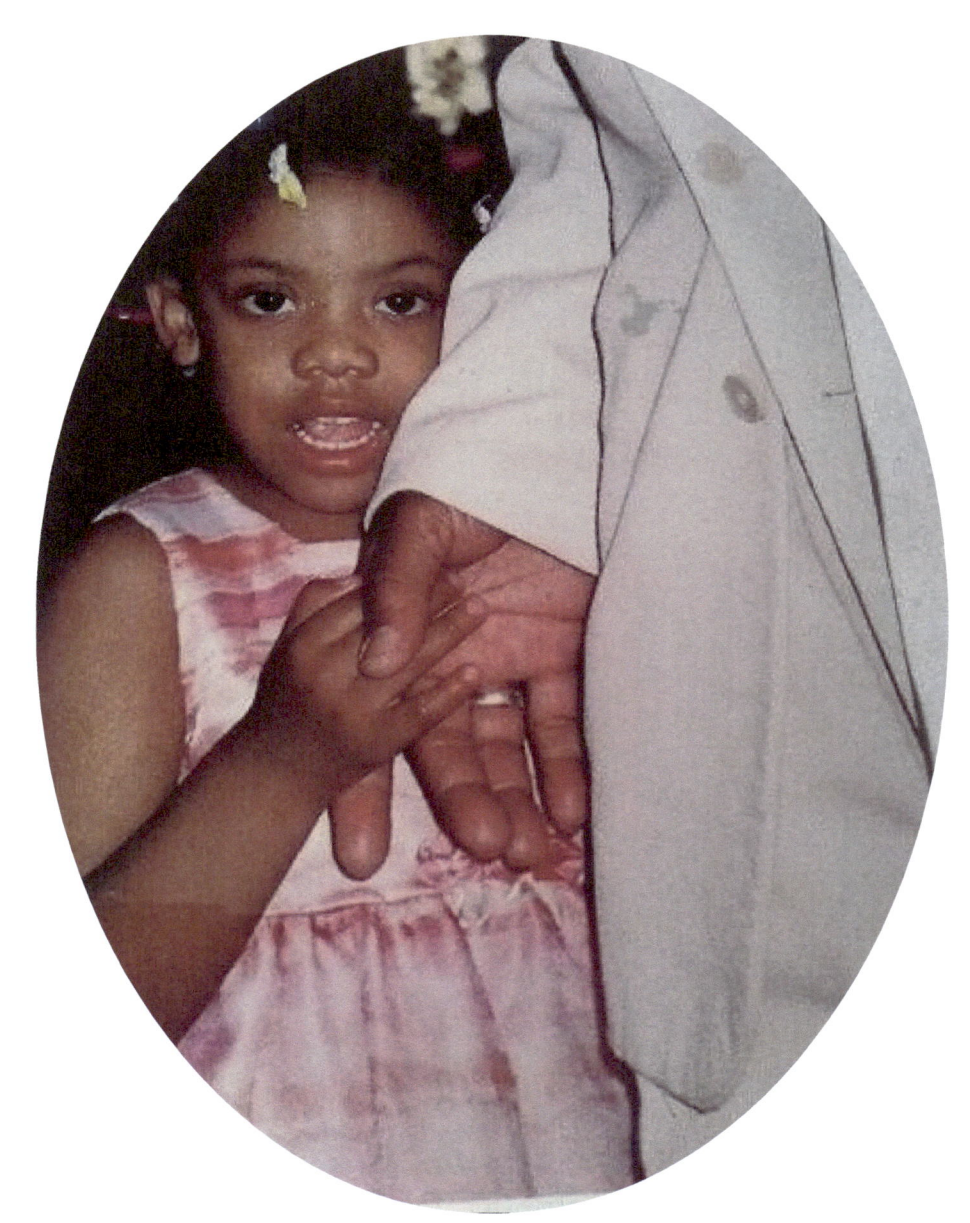

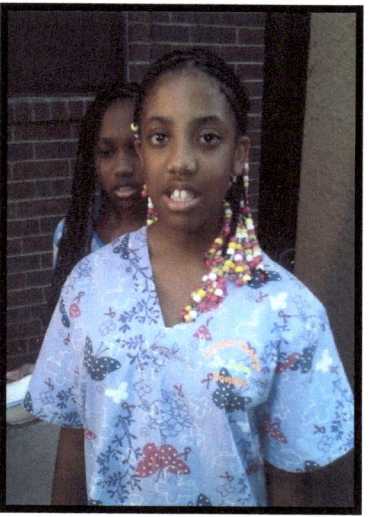

~~The end~~ Dafney

No Dafney, This is The beginning!

Love ya,
Daddy's Girl!

www.ingramcontent.com/pod-product-compliance
Lightning Source LLC
Chambersburg PA
CBHW042116040426
42449CB00002B/66